Africa

Tawanda Tawanda

Published by Tawanda Tawanda, 2024.

Also by Tawanda Tawanda

Life After Divorce
African Child
Purpose of Life
Africa

Description

Africa by Tawanda Tawanda is an illuminating journey through the heart and soul of the African continent. This comprehensive book explores Africa's profound history, breathtaking landscapes, vibrant cultures, and boundless potential.

From the origins of humanity to the modern challenges and triumphs, Africa celebrates the spirit of resilience, innovation, and unity that defines the continent. Delve into the diverse tribes, natural wonders, iconic destinations, and the rich tapestry of arts, cuisine, and traditions that make Africa unique.

The book also examines critical issues such as colonization's lingering effects, environmental challenges, and the role of technology in shaping Africa's future. With an emphasis on collaboration, sustainable development, and the power of Africa's youthful population, this book offers a hopeful vision for the continent's place in the world.

Africa is both an homage to the past and a call to action for a brighter, united future. Whether you are an African seeking to reconnect with your roots or someone curious about the continent's incredible story, this book is an essential read.

Epigraph

"I am because we are, and since we are, therefore I am."

— African Proverb

"Africa has her mysteries, and even a wise man cannot understand them. But a wise man respects them."

— Miriam Makeba

Disclaimer

The information presented in this book is for general knowledge, inspiration, and educational purposes. While every effort has been made to ensure the accuracy and reliability of the content, the author does not guarantee that all information is free from errors or omissions. Readers are encouraged to conduct their own research or seek professional advice when necessary.

The views and opinions expressed in this book are those of the author and do not necessarily reflect those of any organization or entity associated with the author.

This book includes interpretations of historical, cultural, and contemporary topics based on available sources. It is not intended to misrepresent or diminish any individual, community, or nation.

The author disclaims any liability for any loss, damage, or inconvenience caused as a result of using this book. All efforts have been made to present content respectfully and inclusively.

For inquiries or concerns, please contact the author.

Dedication

To the resilient people of Africa,

whose spirit, strength, and stories inspire the world.

To my spiritual father and mother, L. Mangwiro,

for their unwavering guidance and wisdom.

And to the future generations of Africa,

may you rise with pride, courage, and unity

to fulfill the boundless potential of our beloved continent.

This book is for you.

Chapter 1: The Beginning of Africa

Africa, often referred to as the "Cradle of Humanity," holds a unique place in the history of the world. Its story begins millions of years ago, offering profound insights into the origins of humankind, the evolution of civilizations, and the role of its geography and natural resources in shaping the continent's destiny.

The Cradle of Humanity: Origins and Historical Significance

Africa's significance as the birthplace of humanity is rooted in the fossil evidence discovered on the continent. Anthropologists and archaeologists have unearthed remains of some of the earliest hominins, including Australopithecus afarensis, famously represented by the fossil "Lucy," found in Ethiopia. Further discoveries of Homo habilis and Homo erectus in East Africa's Great Rift Valley confirmed the region as the starting point of human evolution.

This remarkable legacy is underscored by Africa's contribution to human ancestry. Genetic studies have revealed that modern humans (Homo sapiens) originated in Africa roughly 200,000 years ago. These early humans began migrating out of the continent around 60,000 years ago, spreading across the globe and forming the foundation of all modern human populations. Africa's role as the "motherland" of humanity places it at the heart of the human story, making its history both unique and universally significant.

Evolution of Civilizations and Early Human Migration

As humanity evolved, so did its capacity to build societies and civilizations. The earliest forms of organized communities emerged along Africa's fertile river valleys, most notably along the Nile. Ancient Egypt, one of the world's first and most influential civilizations, rose to prominence around 3100 BCE. Renowned for its advancements in architecture, mathematics, medicine, and governance, Egypt's impact on human history is immeasurable.

Further south, civilizations like Nubia (Kush) flourished, establishing themselves as powerful centers of trade and culture. To the west, the ancient city of Carthage became a hub of commerce and naval power. Later, sub-Saharan Africa saw the rise of kingdoms such as Ghana, Mali, and Songhai, which dominated trans-Saharan trade routes with their wealth in gold, salt, and knowledge.

The migrations of the Bantu people, beginning around 2000 BCE, also shaped Africa's cultural and linguistic diversity. Spreading from the Niger-Congo region to the rest of sub-Saharan Africa, the Bantu brought innovations in agriculture, metallurgy, and social organization. These movements laid the groundwork for many modern African societies.

Impact of Geography and Natural Resources on Africa's Development

Africa's vast and diverse geography has played a crucial role in its history. Spanning deserts, savannas, rainforests, and mountains, the continent's varied landscapes influenced settlement patterns, trade, and cultural exchanges. The Sahara Desert, for instance, served both as a barrier and a bridge, isolating sub-Saharan Africa while facilitating trade with North Africa and beyond.

Rivers like the Nile, Niger, and Congo became lifelines for early civilizations, providing water, fertile soil, and transportation routes. The Great Rift Valley, with its volcanic activity and tectonic movements, not only shaped the physical landscape but also contributed to the preservation of critical archaeological sites.

Africa's natural wealth has always been a double-edged sword. Rich in resources like gold, diamonds, and oil, the continent has attracted traders and invaders throughout history. Ancient gold mines in southern Africa and the diamond fields of Kimberley are examples of how resources have shaped Africa's global interactions, for better or worse. These resources became the backbone of powerful empires but also a source of exploitation during the colonial era.

Conclusion

The beginning of Africa's story is the beginning of humanity's story. As the cradle of life and the bedrock of early civilizations, Africa's contributions to the world are immeasurable. Its diverse geography and abundant resources have shaped the destiny of its people, offering both immense opportunities and formidable challenges. This rich history sets the stage for understanding the complexities and wonders of modern Africa—a land as ancient as it is dynamic.

Chapter 2: Best Places to Visit in Africa

Africa is a continent of stunning diversity, offering travelers everything from awe-inspiring natural wonders to vibrant cultural experiences. Whether you are drawn to its iconic wildlife, rich history, or breathtaking landscapes, Africa has something for everyone. This chapter provides a detailed guide to the continent's top destinations, along with essential travel tips, cultural etiquettes, and must-see festivals to enhance your journey.

—-

Safari Wonders

1. Serengeti National Park (Tanzania)

The Serengeti is synonymous with African safaris. This UNESCO World Heritage Site is famous for the Great Migration, where millions of wildebeests, zebras, and antelopes traverse the plains in search of greener pastures. Visitors can enjoy game drives to spot the "Big Five" (lion, elephant, buffalo, leopard, and rhinoceros) and experience the untouched beauty of the African savanna.

Best Time to Visit: June to October for the migration; January to February for calving season.

2. Masai Mara National Reserve (Kenya)

Adjacent to the Serengeti, the Masai Mara offers another spectacular safari experience. Known for its abundant wildlife and Maasai culture, visitors can explore the park through hot air balloon rides and guided tours by local Maasai warriors.

Best Time to Visit: July to October for the Great Migration crossing the Mara River.

3. Kruger National Park (South Africa)

One of Africa's largest and most accessible game reserves, Kruger National Park offers self-drive safaris, luxury lodges, and guided tours. The park boasts diverse ecosystems, from savannas to forests, and is home to over 500 bird species and 150 mammal species.

Best Time to Visit: May to September during the dry season.

—-

Cultural Gems

1. Timbuktu (Mali)

Once a thriving center of Islamic scholarship and trade, Timbuktu remains a symbol of Africa's rich history. Visitors can explore ancient mosques like Djinguereber, libraries housing centuries-old manuscripts, and the vibrant local markets.

Travel Tip: Due to recent instability, consult travel advisories and consider guided tours for safety.

2. Zanzibar (Tanzania)

Zanzibar is a tropical paradise with a rich cultural heritage. Stroll through the narrow streets of Stone Town, a UNESCO World Heritage Site, to discover its Swahili-Arabic architecture. Relax on pristine beaches, dive into coral reefs, and visit spice plantations for a sensory adventure.

Best Time to Visit: June to October for dry weather.

3. Marrakech (Morocco)

The "Red City" of Marrakech offers a captivating blend of old and new. Wander through the bustling souks, visit the majestic Koutoubia Mosque, and explore the historic Bahia Palace. Don't miss the vibrant Jemaa el-Fnaa square for street performances and traditional Moroccan food.

Best Time to Visit: March to May or September to November.

—-

Natural Marvels

1. Victoria Falls (Zambia/Zimbabwe)

Known locally as "Mosi-oa-Tunya" (The Smoke That Thunders), Victoria Falls is one of the largest and most spectacular waterfalls in the world. Visitors can enjoy breathtaking views, white-water rafting on the Zambezi River, and helicopter tours for a bird's-eye perspective.

Best Time to Visit: February to May when the falls are at their fullest.

2. Mount Kilimanjaro (Tanzania)

Africa's highest peak, Kilimanjaro, is a dream destination for adventure seekers. The dormant volcano offers various climbing routes suitable for beginners and experienced trekkers. The views from Uhuru Peak, the highest point, are unmatched.

Best Time to Visit: January to March or June to October.

3. Sahara Desert (North Africa)

The world's largest hot desert offers unique experiences, from camel treks across the golden dunes to stargazing under the vast, clear skies. Explore ancient Berber villages and stay in traditional desert camps for an authentic experience.

Best Time to Visit: October to April to avoid extreme heat.

—-

Urban Highlights

1. Cape Town (South Africa)

Nestled between Table Mountain and the Atlantic Ocean, Cape Town is a city of extraordinary beauty. Visit Robben Island, the Kirstenbosch Botanical Gardens, and the Cape Winelands. Don't miss the vibrant neighborhoods of Bo-Kaap and the scenic Cape Point.

Best Time to Visit: November to March for summer weather.

2. Lagos (Nigeria)

Lagos, Africa's most populous city, is a hub of energy and creativity. Enjoy its thriving arts scene, vibrant nightlife, and culinary delights. Visit Lekki Conservation Centre and Nike Art Gallery for a taste of Nigeria's rich culture.

Travel Tip: Embrace the lively pace but plan ahead to navigate traffic.

3. Cairo (Egypt)

Cairo offers a gateway to ancient and modern wonders. Explore the Great Pyramids of Giza, the Egyptian Museum, and the bustling Khan el-Khalili bazaar. A sunset cruise along the Nile is a perfect way to end the day.

Best Time to Visit: October to April.

—-

Travel Tips, Cultural Etiquettes, and Must-See Festivals

Travel Tips:

Always check visa requirements and health advisories for your destination.

Hire local guides to gain deeper insights into the culture and history.

Pack appropriately for the climate and terrain, especially for safaris or desert visits.

Cultural Etiquettes:

Respect local customs and dress modestly, especially in conservative regions.

Learn a few basic phrases in the local language to show respect.

Always ask for permission before photographing people.

Must-See Festivals:

Timkat (Ethiopia): A vibrant Epiphany celebration in January.

Lake of Stars Festival (Malawi): A lively music festival by the lakeside.

Festival of the Sahara (Tunisia): A cultural event showcasing traditional desert life.

Africa's allure lies in its unparalleled diversity. Whether exploring its untamed wilderness, immersing yourself in its rich cultures, or marveling at its natural and urban wonders, each destination offers an unforgettable experience. This chapter highlights only a glimpse of what awaits travelers willing to embrace the continent's magic.

Chapter 3: The Good

Africa is a continent brimming with beauty, strength, and potential. Despite its challenges, it remains a land of incredible cultural richness, natural wealth, and boundless creativity. This chapter explores the "good" of Africa, highlighting its vibrant culture, unparalleled biodiversity, emerging economies, and inspiring stories of resilience and success.

—-

Rich Culture, Music, and Art

Africa's cultural diversity is one of its greatest assets. With over 2,000 languages and countless ethnic groups, the continent is a tapestry of traditions, beliefs, and expressions that have shaped global culture.

1. Music:

African music is the heartbeat of the continent, influencing genres worldwide. The rhythmic beats of the djembe drum, the soulful melodies of Afrobeat pioneers like Fela Kuti, and the modern-day dominance of artists like Burna Boy, Wizkid, and Angelique Kidjo reflect the evolution of African soundscapes. South Africa's jazz scene, Mali's griot tradition, and Congo's soukous music add to this rich mix.

2. Art:

African art is as diverse as its people. From ancient rock paintings in Namibia to the contemporary works of artists like El Anatsui and Wangechi Mutu, the continent's creativity is boundless. Traditional crafts such as beadwork, mask carving, and textile weaving tell stories of ancestry and identity, while modern galleries and biennales, such as the Dakar Biennale, showcase Africa's evolving art scene.

3. Cultural Festivals:

Festivals like Nigeria's Calabar Carnival, Morocco's Mawazine Festival, and Ethiopia's Timkat celebration are a testament to Africa's vibrant cultural life. These events bring people together, showcasing music, dance, fashion, and food that celebrate the continent's diversity.

—-

Biodiversity and Unique Ecosystems

Africa is home to some of the world's most extraordinary wildlife and ecosystems, making it a global biodiversity hotspot.

1. Wildlife:

Africa's "Big Five" (lion, elephant, buffalo, leopard, and rhinoceros) are iconic symbols of the continent's wildlife heritage. National parks like Serengeti, Okavango Delta, and Etosha offer unmatched opportunities to witness these animals in their natural habitats.

2. Unique Ecosystems:

Africa boasts a wide variety of ecosystems, from the lush Congo Rainforest, the second-largest tropical rainforest in the world, to the arid Namib Desert, one of the oldest deserts on Earth. The Great Rift Valley is another marvel, home to unique geological formations and rich biodiversity.

3. Conservation Efforts:

Despite threats like poaching and climate change, Africa leads in conservation initiatives. Projects such as Kenya's elephant corridors, Rwanda's mountain gorilla conservation, and South Africa's rhino protection efforts are helping to safeguard the continent's natural heritage for future generations.

—-

Emerging Economies and Innovation Hubs

Africa is a land of immense economic potential. In recent decades, several countries have emerged as engines of growth and innovation.

1. Economic Growth:

Nations like Nigeria, South Africa, Kenya, and Ethiopia are driving the continent's economy, supported by sectors like agriculture, mining, manufacturing, and services. The African Continental Free Trade Area (AfCFTA), the world's largest free trade zone, is set to boost intra-African trade and economic integration.

2. Innovation Hubs:

Silicon Savannah (Kenya): Nairobi is leading Africa's tech revolution, with innovations like M-Pesa, a mobile money service that has transformed financial inclusion.

Nigeria: Lagos has become a hub for fintech startups and creative industries, particularly Nollywood and Afrobeats.

South Africa: Known for its advanced financial sector, Cape Town and Johannesburg also host thriving tech ecosystems.

3. Renewable Energy:

Africa is harnessing its abundant solar and wind resources to power its future. Countries like Morocco, with its Noor Ouarzazate Solar Complex, and South Africa are investing in green energy solutions.

—-

Examples of African Resilience and Success Stories

The spirit of resilience defines Africa. Despite historical and modern challenges, individuals and communities continue to rise, creating inspiring success stories.

1. Nelson Mandela and Post-Apartheid South Africa:

Mandela's journey from political prisoner to president symbolizes the triumph of hope and reconciliation over division. His leadership helped South Africa transition from apartheid to democracy, inspiring global movements for justice.

2. Wangari Maathai and Environmental Activism:

The Kenyan Nobel Laureate founded the Green Belt Movement, empowering women to plant millions of trees, combat deforestation, and promote sustainable development.

3. Rwanda's Recovery:

After the 1994 genocide, Rwanda emerged as a model of reconciliation and progress. Today, it boasts one of the fastest-growing economies in Africa, clean cities like Kigali, and groundbreaking initiatives in gender equality and technology.

4. Youth-Led Innovations:

Across Africa, young entrepreneurs are solving local problems with global impact. Ugandan innovator Brian Gitta developed Matibabu, a device for diagnosing malaria without blood tests. Nigerian entrepreneur Temie Giwa-Tubosun founded LifeBank, a startup revolutionizing blood delivery to hospitals.

5. Cultural Exports:

Africa's influence on global culture continues to grow. From Hollywood's adoption of African narratives (e.g., Black Panther) to the global popularity of Afrobeat and African fashion, the continent's soft power is undeniable.

—-

Conclusion

Africa's "good" is vast and undeniable. Its rich culture, breathtaking biodiversity, and rising economies paint a picture of a continent full of promise and vitality. African resilience, creativity, and innovation demonstrate the strength and potential of its people. While challenges persist, these stories of triumph and progress remind us of the boundless opportunities that lie within Africa's borders. This is the Africa that the world needs to know and celebrate.

Chapter 4: The Bad

Africa's history and contemporary challenges reveal a complex narrative of struggles and setbacks that continue to shape the continent. While Africa is a land of immense potential and resilience, it faces significant obstacles rooted in its past and present. This chapter explores the darker aspects of Africa's story, including the lingering effects of colonization, challenges like poverty, corruption, and political instability, as well as environmental degradation and climate change.

—-

Historical Colonization and Its Lingering Effects

The colonial era, spanning the late 19th and early 20th centuries, left indelible scars on Africa. European powers divided the continent during the infamous Berlin Conference of 1884-1885, disregarding existing cultural, linguistic, and tribal boundaries. This division sowed seeds of conflict and disunity that persist to this day.

1. Exploitation of Resources:

Colonizers extracted vast quantities of Africa's natural wealth—gold, diamonds, oil, and more—without benefiting local populations. Infrastructure was built primarily to serve colonial interests, such as transporting resources to ports, rather than fostering development for Africans.

2. Displacement and Oppression:

Millions of Africans were displaced from their ancestral lands, and entire societies were disrupted. Colonial administrations imposed exploitative systems like forced labor and high taxation, leading to widespread suffering.

3. Cultural Erosion:

Indigenous languages, traditions, and systems of governance were often suppressed in favor of European customs. This cultural disruption created identity crises that still affect many African societies.

4. Legacy of Arbitrary Borders:

The artificial borders drawn by colonial powers ignored ethnic and cultural realities, creating tensions among groups forced to share the same state. This has led to numerous conflicts, including civil wars in countries like Sudan and the Democratic Republic of Congo.

—-

Challenges: Poverty, Corruption, and Political Instability

Africa's potential is often undermined by systemic challenges that hinder progress and development.

1. Poverty:

Despite its natural wealth, Africa remains the poorest continent in terms of GDP per capita. Many African nations struggle with inadequate healthcare, education, and basic infrastructure.

Rural communities are often the hardest hit, with limited access to clean water, electricity, and modern farming techniques.

Urban areas face issues like overcrowding in slums and high unemployment rates.

2. Corruption:

Corruption is a significant barrier to development in many African countries. Mismanagement of public funds, embezzlement, and bribery divert resources away from essential services.

High-profile scandals, such as South Africa's state capture case, highlight the systemic nature of corruption.

Corruption also deters foreign investment, as businesses are wary of operating in unstable environments.

3. Political Instability:

Political instability, often fueled by ethnic divisions, weak institutions, and external interference, has plagued many African nations.

Military coups, such as those seen in Mali and Sudan, disrupt democratic processes.

Prolonged conflicts, like those in Somalia and Libya, create power vacuums that are exploited by extremist groups.

Lack of trust in governance leads to widespread disillusionment among citizens.

—-

Environmental Degradation and Climate Change Issues

Africa's environment is both a source of life and a cause of concern. Environmental degradation, combined with the effects of climate change, threatens the continent's ecosystems and livelihoods.

1. Deforestation and Land Degradation:

Forests, including the Congo Rainforest, are being destroyed at alarming rates due to logging, agriculture, and urbanization.

Overgrazing and poor land management contribute to soil erosion, reducing agricultural productivity and causing desertification.

2. Water Scarcity:

Many African countries face water shortages, exacerbated by population growth and poor infrastructure.

The Nile, a vital water source, is under increasing pressure due to upstream dam projects and climate change.

3. Wildlife Threats:

Poaching and habitat loss endanger Africa's iconic species, including elephants, rhinos, and lions.

Illegal wildlife trade not only depletes biodiversity but also undermines conservation efforts.

4. Climate Change Impacts:

Rising temperatures and erratic rainfall patterns are affecting agriculture, a critical sector for many African economies.

Coastal communities face threats from rising sea levels, particularly in West Africa.

Extreme weather events, such as droughts and floods, are becoming more frequent, leading to food insecurity and displacement.

—-

Conclusion

The challenges facing Africa are daunting and deeply rooted in history and systemic issues. The legacy of colonization continues to shape the continent's political and social landscape, while poverty, corruption, and instability hinder progress. Environmental degradation and climate change further compound these problems, threatening the livelihoods of millions.

However, acknowledging these challenges is the first step toward finding solutions. Africa's struggles are not insurmountable; they are opportunities for transformation. By addressing these issues head-on, Africa can overcome its past and present obstacles to unlock a brighter future.

Chapter 5: The Diverse Tribes of Africa

Africa is a continent renowned for its rich cultural diversity, much of which is rooted in its myriad tribes. With over 3,000 ethnic groups speaking more than 2,000 languages, the tribal communities of Africa are a cornerstone of the continent's identity. This chapter explores some of the major tribes, delves into their traditions, languages, and unique practices, and examines the crucial role tribes play in shaping Africa's cultural identity.

—-

Overview of Major Tribes

1. Zulu (South Africa)

The Zulu are one of the largest and most well-known tribes in Africa, numbering approximately 10 million people. They are predominantly found in South Africa's KwaZulu-Natal province.

Language: The Zulu speak isiZulu, a Bantu language and one of South Africa's official languages.

Traditions: Zulu culture is deeply rooted in storytelling, dance, and ceremonies, including the famous umemulo (coming-of-age ceremony).

Historical Significance: The Zulu Kingdom, under leaders like Shaka Zulu, played a pivotal role in Southern African history.

2. Maasai (Kenya and Tanzania)

The Maasai are semi-nomadic people known for their distinctive customs and dress. They inhabit the savannas of Kenya and Tanzania.

Language: The Maasai speak Maa, a Nilotic language, as well as Swahili and English.

Unique Practices: Cattle are central to Maasai life, serving as a measure of wealth and a source of food and status. Traditional ceremonies, such as the jumping dance (adumu), showcase their vibrant culture.

Tourism: The Maasai are a symbol of East African culture and often participate in cultural tourism.

3. Yoruba (Nigeria, Benin, Togo)

The Yoruba are one of the largest ethnic groups in Africa, primarily found in Nigeria and neighboring countries.

Language: Yoruba is both a language and a culture, and it is widely spoken in Nigeria.

Traditions: Yoruba religion, which includes the worship of deities called Orisha, has influenced the African diaspora in the Americas, particularly in Brazil and Cuba.

Art and Literature: The Yoruba are known for their rich artistic traditions, including beadwork, sculpture, and storytelling.

4. Berbers (North Africa)

The Berbers, also known as Amazigh, are indigenous to North Africa, particularly in Morocco, Algeria, and Libya.

Language: The Berber languages belong to the Afro-Asiatic family, with Tamazight being one of the most widely spoken.

Unique Practices: The Berbers have maintained their traditions through music, festivals, and craftsmanship, particularly in weaving and jewelry.

Cultural Resilience: Despite Arabization in North Africa, the Berbers have preserved their identity and language, with increasing recognition of their rights in recent years.

5. Hausa (West Africa)

The Hausa are one of the largest ethnic groups in West Africa, primarily found in Nigeria, Niger, and Ghana.

Language: Hausa is one of the most widely spoken languages in Africa and serves as a lingua franca in West Africa.

Traditions: Hausa culture is strongly influenced by Islam, which is reflected in their art, architecture, and festivals like Durbar, a grand horse-riding celebration.

6. San (Southern Africa)

The San, also known as Bushmen, are indigenous hunter-gatherers of Southern Africa.

Language: San languages are characterized by unique click sounds.

Unique Practices: The San are known for their deep knowledge of the environment, including tracking and survival skills.

Challenges: Modernization and land rights issues have significantly impacted their way of life.

—-

Traditions, Languages, and Unique Practices

1. Oral Traditions:

Storytelling is a vital tradition across African tribes, used to pass down history, morals, and cultural values. Griots, or oral historians, play a crucial role in preserving and sharing these stories.

2. Ceremonies and Rites:

Many tribes have elaborate ceremonies for life events such as births, marriages, and funerals. For example, the Xhosa practice ulwaluko, a rite of passage for boys into manhood, while the Dogon tribe in Mali performs elaborate funeral dances.

3. Clothing and Adornments:

The Maasai wear brightly colored shúkà (cloaks) and elaborate beadwork.

The Himba women in Namibia coat their skin with otjize, a mixture of butterfat and red ochre, as both a beauty practice and protection from the sun.

The Tuareg people of the Sahara are known as the "Blue People" due to the indigo-dyed garments they wear.

4. Languages:

Africa's linguistic diversity is unparalleled. Bantu languages dominate Southern and Central Africa, while Nilotic, Afro-Asiatic, and Nilo-Saharan languages are prominent in other regions. Some tribes, like the Khoisan-speaking San, have languages with unique phonetic features, such as clicks.

—-

Role of Tribes in Shaping Africa's Cultural Identity

1. Cultural Preservation:

Tribes act as custodians of traditions, ensuring that Africa's rich heritage is preserved despite modern influences. From traditional medicine to artisanal crafts, tribal knowledge remains integral to African identity.

2. Community and Social Structure:

Tribal affiliations often define social structures, providing a sense of belonging and responsibility. Elders play a significant role in decision-making and conflict resolution, emphasizing collective well-being.

3. Influence on Modern Culture:

Tribal traditions have influenced modern African culture, from fashion to music. Tribal patterns, for instance, inspire contemporary designs, while Afrobeat music incorporates traditional rhythms.

4. Tourism and Global Recognition:

Tribes are central to Africa's cultural tourism, attracting visitors eager to experience traditional dances, ceremonies, and crafts. This not only promotes cultural appreciation but also supports local economies.

—-

Conclusion

The diverse tribes of Africa are the heartbeat of the continent, embodying its history, traditions, and values. Each tribe contributes to the mosaic that is African identity, offering unique languages, practices, and stories that enrich the world. While modernity presents challenges to preserving tribal customs, these communities remain resilient, adapting to change while staying rooted in their heritage. Through their enduring presence, Africa's tribes continue to inspire and shape the cultural narrative of the continent.

Chapter 6: The Role of Women in Africa

Women have always been at the heart of African societies, shaping the continent's history, culture, and progress. From their roles in traditional societies to their leadership in modern times, African women have demonstrated remarkable resilience, strength, and ingenuity. This chapter explores the historical and modern roles of women, celebrates notable female leaders and change-makers, and examines the challenges they face in the pursuit of gender equality.

—-

Historical Roles of Women in African Societies

In traditional African societies, women held significant roles that extended beyond the household.

1. Caretakers and Educators:

Women were the primary caregivers, ensuring the well-being of their families and educating children in cultural values and traditions.

2. Economic Contributors:

In agricultural societies, women played a crucial role in farming, food production, and trade.

In pastoralist communities, women managed livestock and contributed to the economy through their labor and skills.

3. Spiritual Leaders:

Women often served as priestesses, diviners, and custodians of spiritual knowledge. In many tribes, they were seen as intermediaries between the human and spiritual realms.

4. Warriors and Leaders:

Queen Nzinga of Ndongo and Matamba (present-day Angola) is celebrated for her military leadership and resistance against Portuguese colonization.

Yaa Asantewaa of the Ashanti Empire (Ghana) led a rebellion against British imperialism in the late 19th century.

—-

Modern Roles of Women in African Society

In contemporary Africa, women continue to make significant strides, taking on roles in governance, business, education, and activism.

1. Political Leadership:

Ellen Johnson Sirleaf of Liberia became Africa's first elected female president, serving as an inspiration for women in leadership.

Ngozi Okonjo-Iweala of Nigeria is a trailblazer in global economics, serving as the Director-General of the World Trade Organization.

2. Economic Participation:

Women drive informal economies across Africa, running small businesses, trading in markets, and engaging in agriculture.

Female entrepreneurs like Bethlehem Tilahun Alemu (founder of SoleRebels in Ethiopia) have gained international recognition for creating sustainable businesses.

3. Education and Advocacy:

Women are leading efforts to improve access to education, particularly for girls. Organizations like the Malala Fund and CAMFED (Campaign for Female Education) work closely with African women leaders to uplift communities.

4. Arts and Culture:

African women are prominent in arts, literature, and entertainment. Writers like Chimamanda Ngozi Adichie (Nigeria) and filmmakers like Wanuri Kahiu (Kenya) challenge societal norms and tell African stories on a global stage.

—-

Celebrating Female Leaders, Activists, and Entrepreneurs

African women have made remarkable contributions in various fields, inspiring change and progress.

1. Leaders in Politics and Governance:

Joyce Banda (Malawi): Africa's second female president, advocating for women's empowerment and social development.

Graça Machel (Mozambique and South Africa): A global advocate for women and children's rights.

2. Activists:

Wangari Maathai (Kenya): Nobel Peace Prize laureate and founder of the Green Belt Movement, promoting environmental conservation and women's rights.

Funmilayo Ransome-Kuti (Nigeria): A feminist and activist who fought for women's voting rights and social justice.

3. Entrepreneurs:

Folorunsho Alakija (Nigeria): One of Africa's richest women, known for her success in the oil, fashion, and real estate industries.

Tabitha Karanja (Kenya): Founder of Keroche Breweries, breaking barriers in a male-dominated industry.

—-

Challenges Women Face in Africa

Despite their contributions, African women face significant challenges that hinder their full potential.

1. Gender-Based Violence:

Women in Africa experience high rates of domestic violence, sexual assault, and harmful practices like female genital mutilation (FGM) and child marriage.

Activists and organizations, such as Equality Now and the African Women's Development Fund, are working to combat these issues.

2. Economic Inequality:

Women are often excluded from formal economic opportunities, with limited access to land ownership, credit, and financial resources.

Gender pay gaps persist, even in sectors where women form the majority of the workforce.

3. Limited Political Representation:

While progress has been made, women remain underrepresented in political leadership across the continent.

Traditional patriarchal norms often discourage women from pursuing careers in politics.

4. Access to Education:

In many rural areas, girls face barriers to education, including early marriage, poverty, and cultural expectations.

Initiatives like the African Girls' Education Initiative aim to improve literacy and school attendance rates among girls.

5. Healthcare Disparities:

Women face challenges in accessing quality healthcare, particularly maternal and reproductive health services.

High maternal mortality rates remain a critical issue in sub-Saharan Africa.

—-

Steps Toward Gender Equality

Efforts to empower African women and promote gender equality are gaining momentum.

1. Policy Changes:

Governments are enacting laws to protect women's rights, such as banning FGM and increasing quotas for women in political offices.

Initiatives like the Maputo Protocol on Women's Rights provide a framework for advancing gender equality.

2. Education Initiatives:

Programs like Educate Girls and UNICEF's Girls' Education campaign are helping bridge the gender gap in education.

3. Economic Empowerment:

Microfinance institutions and organizations like the Grameen Foundation provide women with access to credit and resources to start businesses.

Skills training programs enable women to participate in various industries, from agriculture to technology.

4. Community Advocacy:

Grassroots organizations, often led by women, are working to address cultural norms and practices that hinder women's progress.

Men are also being engaged in conversations about gender equality to foster mutual understanding and support.

—

Conclusion

The role of women in Africa is a story of resilience, strength, and untapped potential. Historically, women have been integral to African societies, contributing as caregivers, leaders, and spiritual guides. In modern times, they continue to break barriers and shape the continent's future in politics, business, and advocacy.

However, challenges persist, from gender-based violence to economic and educational disparities. By addressing these issues and promoting gender equality, Africa can unlock the full potential of its women, fostering progress and prosperity for all. The empowerment of women is not just a moral imperative—it is a key to the continent's sustainable development.

Chapter 7: Africa's Natural Resources

Africa is a continent of extraordinary natural wealth, holding vast reserves of gold, diamonds, oil, rare earth minerals, and other valuable resources. These riches have the potential to drive economic growth and improve livelihoods across the continent. However, they have also been at the heart of many conflicts, environmental degradation, and economic challenges, a phenomenon often referred to as the "resource curse." This chapter explores the abundance of Africa's natural resources, the complexities of resource management, and the lessons learned from successes and failures across the continent.

—-

The Abundance of Natural Resources

Africa is one of the richest continents in terms of natural resources, which are distributed across its vast and varied landscapes.

1. Gold:

Africa produces nearly 22% of the world's gold, with major deposits in South Africa, Ghana, Mali, and Sudan.

South Africa's Witwatersrand Basin has been one of the most productive gold-mining regions globally, though its output has declined in recent years.

2. Diamonds:

The continent accounts for about 65% of the world's diamond production, with Botswana, Angola, and the Democratic Republic of Congo (DRC) leading the way.

Botswana's diamond industry has been a cornerstone of its economic success, contributing significantly to GDP and infrastructure development.

3. Oil:

Africa holds substantial oil reserves, with Nigeria, Angola, Algeria, and Libya among the largest producers.

Nigeria is the largest oil producer in Africa, with its economy heavily reliant on petroleum exports.

4. Rare Earth Minerals:

The DRC is the world's leading supplier of cobalt, a key component in batteries for electric vehicles and electronics.

Africa also holds significant reserves of lithium, graphite, and other critical minerals needed for renewable energy technologies.

5. Other Resources:

Africa is rich in copper (Zambia, DRC), platinum (South Africa), uranium (Niger, Namibia), and timber (Gabon, Cameroon).

Its agricultural resources, including cocoa (Ivory Coast, Ghana) and coffee (Ethiopia, Uganda), also play a vital role in global markets.

—-

Economic Potential and the "Resource Curse"

While Africa's resources have the potential to transform economies, they have also led to numerous challenges, often referred to collectively as the "resource curse."

1. The Resource Curse:

Countries rich in natural resources often experience slower economic growth, corruption, and conflict compared to those without such wealth.

Over-reliance on resource exports can lead to economic instability, as seen in Nigeria's vulnerability to fluctuating oil prices.

Poor governance and mismanagement of resource revenues exacerbate inequality and underdevelopment.

2. Conflict and Exploitation:

Resources have fueled numerous conflicts, such as the "blood diamonds" that funded civil wars in Sierra Leone and Liberia.

The control of lucrative mining areas has led to violence and exploitation, particularly in the DRC.

3. Environmental Impact:

Resource extraction often results in deforestation, water pollution, and habitat destruction.

Oil spills in the Niger Delta have devastated local ecosystems and livelihoods.

4. Missed Opportunities:

Many African countries export raw materials without adding value through processing or manufacturing, losing out on economic benefits.

The lack of diversification in resource-dependent economies makes them susceptible to external shocks.

Case Studies of Resource Management Successes and Failures

1. Success Stories:

Botswana's Diamond Industry:

Botswana has managed its diamond wealth effectively, creating a sovereign wealth fund and investing in healthcare, education, and infrastructure. The country has avoided the corruption and conflict often associated with resource wealth.

Ghana's Gold Sector:

Ghana has implemented policies to regulate artisanal and small-scale mining, reducing illegal mining and environmental damage while boosting revenues.

2. Failures:

Nigeria's Oil Dependency:

Despite being Africa's largest oil producer, Nigeria has struggled with corruption, environmental degradation, and underdevelopment. Oil wealth has not translated into widespread prosperity, and communities in the Niger Delta suffer from pollution and poverty.

DRC's Cobalt Mining:

The DRC's vast cobalt reserves have been a double-edged sword. While they hold significant economic potential, the mining sector has been plagued by child labor, corruption, and conflict.

—-

Strategies for Sustainable Resource Management

To unlock the full potential of its resources, Africa must adopt strategies that ensure sustainability, equity, and long-term growth.

1. Good Governance and Transparency:

Initiatives like the Extractive Industries Transparency Initiative (EITI) promote accountability and transparency in resource management.

Governments must ensure that revenues are used for public benefit, rather than being siphoned off through corruption.

2. Economic Diversification:

Reducing reliance on resource exports by developing other sectors, such as manufacturing, technology, and tourism, can create more stable economies.

Investing in value-added industries, such as refining crude oil or processing raw minerals, can boost local economies and create jobs.

3. Environmental Protection:

Enforcing environmental regulations and adopting sustainable mining practices can minimize ecological damage.

Rehabilitating mining sites and investing in renewable energy can ensure long-term environmental sustainability.

4. Community Engagement:

Local communities must be involved in resource management decisions to ensure that they benefit from extraction activities.

Revenue-sharing agreements can provide funding for education, healthcare, and infrastructure in resource-rich regions.

5. Regional Cooperation:

Collaborative initiatives, such as the African Mining Vision (AMV), aim to harmonize resource management policies and promote shared prosperity.

—-

Conclusion

Africa's natural resources are a source of immense wealth and opportunity, but they are also a source of significant challenges. The continent's ability to harness these resources for sustainable development depends on effective governance, environmental stewardship, and inclusive economic policies.

By learning from both successes and failures, Africa can break free from the resource curse and leverage its natural wealth to build resilient economies and uplift its people. The key lies in transforming resource extraction from a source of conflict and inequality into a driver of shared prosperity and sustainable development.

Chapter 8: Technology in Africa

Technology is rapidly transforming Africa, revolutionizing industries, economies, and daily life. Innovations in fintech, e-commerce, agriculture, and other sectors are driving progress, while the continent is becoming increasingly influential in global technology trends. However, challenges such as digital literacy, infrastructure gaps, and affordability remain obstacles to widespread tech adoption. This chapter explores the current state of technology in Africa, its innovations, global impact, and the hurdles that need to be overcome for a fully digitized future.

—-

Innovations in African Technology

1. Fintech (Financial Technology):

Africa has become a global leader in fintech innovation, addressing the continent's challenges with traditional banking systems.

Mobile Money:

M-Pesa (Kenya): Launched in 2007, M-Pesa revolutionized mobile banking by enabling users to transfer money, pay bills, and access loans via mobile phones.

The model has been replicated across Africa, transforming economies and empowering millions, especially in rural areas.

Fintech Startups:

Startups like Flutterwave (Nigeria) and Chipper Cash (Ghana) are enabling seamless cross-border payments and financial inclusion.

Cryptocurrency:

Countries like South Africa, Nigeria, and Kenya are witnessing a surge in cryptocurrency usage for remittances and investments.

2. E-Commerce:

Platforms like Jumia (Nigeria) and Takealot (South Africa) are making online shopping accessible to millions, creating a digital marketplace for local businesses.

Social commerce, driven by platforms like WhatsApp and Instagram, is thriving, allowing small businesses to reach wider audiences.

3. Agricultural Technology (AgriTech):

Agriculture remains a backbone of African economies, and technology is enhancing productivity and sustainability.

Precision Farming:

Drone technology and satellite imaging are helping farmers optimize crop yields and manage resources.

Mobile Solutions:

Platforms like Hello Tractor (Nigeria) connect smallholder farmers with tractor owners, improving access to mechanized farming.

Apps like Esoko (Ghana) provide real-time market prices, weather updates, and farming tips.

Sustainability:

Innovations in irrigation and soil management are addressing challenges like water scarcity and desertification.

4. Healthcare Technology (HealthTech):

Startups like Zipline (Rwanda) use drones to deliver medical supplies to remote areas, revolutionizing healthcare delivery.

Mobile apps and telemedicine platforms are improving access to doctors and medical information, especially in underserved regions.

5. Education Technology (EdTech):

Platforms like uLesson (Nigeria) and Eneza Education (Kenya) are providing online learning resources to students across the continent.

Digital classrooms and remote learning initiatives are bridging education gaps in rural areas.

—-

Africa's Role in Global Technology Trends

1. Emerging as a Tech Hub:

Africa is home to vibrant tech ecosystems, with cities like Nairobi (Silicon Savannah), Lagos, and Cape Town emerging as innovation hubs.

The African tech startup scene is attracting significant investment, with venture capital funding exceeding $5 billion in recent years.

2. Youth and Innovation:

Africa's young population is a driving force behind its technological advancements.

Coding bootcamps, innovation hubs, and hackathons are empowering the next generation of tech leaders.

3. Global Partnerships:

Partnerships with global tech giants like Google, Microsoft, and Huawei are fueling digital transformation across Africa.

Initiatives like Facebook's 2Africa project aim to enhance internet connectivity with a subsea cable encircling the continent.

4. Tech Solutions for Global Challenges:

African innovations are addressing global challenges, such as climate change, by developing renewable energy technologies and sustainable agricultural practices.

Startups are creating scalable solutions that can be adapted to other regions, showcasing Africa's potential as a global innovator.

—-

Challenges in Tech Adoption and Digital Literacy

1. Infrastructure Gaps:

Limited access to electricity and reliable internet remains a major barrier, especially in rural areas.

Only about 40% of Africans have access to the internet, compared to a global average of 66%.

2. Digital Literacy:

Many Africans lack the skills needed to fully utilize digital tools, limiting the potential of technology.

Initiatives to promote digital education, particularly for women and marginalized communities, are essential.

3. Affordability:

High costs of smartphones, data, and internet access hinder widespread adoption.

Governments and private sector players must collaborate to make technology affordable and accessible.

4. Policy and Regulation:

Inconsistent regulations and a lack of data protection laws create challenges for tech companies and users.

Governments need to foster a conducive environment for innovation while protecting consumers' rights.

5. Cybersecurity Risks:

The rapid growth of technology has led to increased cyber threats, including fraud and data breaches.

Building robust cybersecurity frameworks is essential to ensure trust and safety in the digital space.

—-

Opportunities for Growth

Despite the challenges, the potential for technology in Africa is immense.

1. Expanding Internet Connectivity:

Investments in infrastructure, such as fiber optic networks and satellite internet, can bring more people online.

Projects like Starlink (Elon Musk's satellite internet initiative) hold promise for connecting remote areas.

2. Promoting Innovation:

Governments and private organizations can support tech startups through funding, mentorship, and incubation programs.

Encouraging local solutions to local problems can drive sustainable development.

3. Fostering Public-Private Partnerships:

Collaboration between governments, businesses, and NGOs can accelerate the adoption of technology in critical sectors like healthcare, education, and agriculture.

4. Building Digital Skills:

Initiatives like the African Digital Skills Fund and Microsoft's Africa Development Center are helping to close the digital skills gap.

Empowering women and youth with digital literacy can unlock untapped potential.

—-

Conclusion

Technology is reshaping Africa, offering unprecedented opportunities for growth, innovation, and development. From fintech to agriculture, African solutions are solving some of the continent's most pressing challenges while contributing to global technology trends.

However, addressing infrastructure gaps, improving digital literacy, and creating inclusive policies are critical to ensuring that no one is left behind in the digital revolution. By investing in technology and fostering innovation, Africa can harness its potential to lead in the 21st century, creating a brighter future for its people and inspiring the world with its ingenuity and resilience.

Chapter 9: Africa's Future

Africa stands on the cusp of transformative change, poised to redefine its global role in the 21st century. With a young and dynamic population, rapid urbanization, and a wealth of untapped potential, the continent's future is brimming with promise. Guided by initiatives like the African Union's Agenda 2063, Africa is charting a course toward inclusive growth, sustainable development, and global leadership. This chapter delves into Africa's aspirations for the future, predictions about its population and urban growth, and the vital role of youth in shaping the continent's destiny.

—-

The African Union's Agenda 2063

The African Union (AU) introduced Agenda 2063 as a strategic framework for achieving Africa's long-term socio-economic transformation. Envisioned as a "blueprint for Africa's development," Agenda 2063 builds on the Pan-African vision of "an integrated, prosperous, and peaceful Africa, driven by its own citizens and representing a dynamic force in the global arena."

1. Key Aspirations of Agenda 2063:

A Prosperous Africa:

Achieving inclusive growth and sustainable development through industrialization, economic diversification, and innovation.

Integrated Continent:

Creating a unified Africa with free movement of people, goods, and services through initiatives like the African Continental Free Trade Area (AfCFTA).

Good Governance and Human Rights:

Promoting democracy, rule of law, and respect for human rights across the continent.

Peace and Security:

Silencing the guns by resolving conflicts and addressing the root causes of instability.

Cultural Renaissance:

Promoting African cultural heritage, languages, and values as tools for unity and pride.

2. Flagship Projects:

AfCFTA:

The world's largest free trade area aims to boost intra-African trade and create a single market for goods and services.

African High-Speed Rail Network:

Connecting major cities across the continent to enhance mobility and trade.

Grand Inga Dam Project:

Harnessing the Congo River's potential to provide electricity to millions and support industrialization.

Pan-African e-Network:

Enhancing digital connectivity and access to education, healthcare, and government services.

—-

Predictions About Population Growth and Urbanization

Africa's demographic trends are set to shape its future profoundly, presenting both opportunities and challenges.

1. Population Growth:

Africa's population is expected to double by 2050, reaching approximately 2.5 billion people.

By 2100, four of the world's most populous countries could be in Africa: Nigeria, Ethiopia, DR Congo, and Egypt.

The growing population offers a vast workforce and consumer base but also raises concerns about resource allocation, employment, and infrastructure.

2. Urbanization:

Africa is urbanizing faster than any other continent, with nearly 60% of its population projected to live in cities by 2050.

Megacities like Lagos, Cairo, Kinshasa, and Johannesburg are growing rapidly, while new urban centers are emerging across the continent.

Urbanization drives economic growth, innovation, and cultural exchange but also exacerbates challenges like housing shortages, traffic congestion, and environmental degradation.

3. Youthful Population:

Over 60% of Africa's population is under the age of 25, making it the youngest continent in the world.

This demographic dividend has the potential to drive economic growth, innovation, and social transformation if adequately harnessed.

—-

The Role of Youth in Driving Change

Africa's youth are its greatest asset, brimming with energy, creativity, and resilience. As future leaders, entrepreneurs, and innovators, young Africans hold the key to the continent's development.

1. Youth in Technology and Innovation:

The tech-savvy younger generation is leading Africa's digital transformation.

Startups in fintech, e-commerce, and edtech are addressing local challenges and attracting global attention.

Coding bootcamps, innovation hubs, and mentorship programs are empowering youth to create solutions for Africa's future.

2. Youth and Governance:

Young Africans are demanding accountability, transparency, and inclusivity in governance.

Movements like #EndSARS (Nigeria) and #FeesMustFall (South Africa) demonstrate the power of youth-led activism in driving social and political change.

Youth participation in politics is growing, with younger leaders emerging across the continent.

3. Youth in Entrepreneurship:

Africa's youth are embracing entrepreneurship as a path to self-reliance and economic empowerment.

Initiatives like the Tony Elumelu Foundation and Anzisha Prize are nurturing young entrepreneurs and providing access to funding and networks.

4. Education and Skills Development:

Investments in education and vocational training are essential to equip youth with the skills needed for the 21st-century workforce.

Emphasizing STEM (Science, Technology, Engineering, and Mathematics) education can drive innovation and industrialization.

—

Opportunities and Challenges

1. Opportunities:

Economic Growth:

A young and growing population can drive economic productivity and consumer spending.

Innovation:

Youth-driven innovation can address Africa's challenges and position the continent as a global leader in technology and sustainability.

Cultural Renaissance:

The younger generation can preserve and promote African heritage while embracing modernity.

2. Challenges:

Unemployment:

High youth unemployment rates threaten social stability and economic progress.

Education Gaps:

Limited access to quality education and skills training hampers youth potential.

Climate Change:

Rapid urbanization and population growth exacerbate environmental challenges, requiring sustainable solutions.

—-

Africa's Global Role in the Future

Africa's future is not just a regional concern but a global one. As the continent becomes increasingly integrated into the global economy, its influence will grow in areas such as:

Trade and Commerce:

With initiatives like AfCFTA, Africa is poised to become a major player in global trade.

Cultural Diplomacy:

African art, music, fashion, and cuisine are gaining global recognition, enhancing the continent's soft power.

Sustainability:

Africa's vast natural resources and renewable energy potential can contribute to global efforts to combat climate change.

Geopolitics:

A united and prosperous Africa can wield significant influence in international organizations and negotiations.

—

Conclusion

Africa's future is full of possibilities, shaped by its ambitious vision, youthful energy, and abundant resources. While challenges like unemployment, governance, and climate change persist, the continent's resilience and determination offer hope for a brighter tomorrow.

By investing in education, technology, and inclusive policies, Africa can unlock its full potential and take its rightful place as a leader on the global stage. The road ahead may be complex, but with unity, innovation, and visionary leadership, Africa's future is one of boundless opportunity and promise.

Chapter 10: Africa and the World

Africa's relationship with the rest of the world is multifaceted, shaped by centuries of trade, cultural exchange, colonialism, and contemporary geopolitical dynamics. As the continent emerges as a global player in economic, political, and cultural spheres, its interactions with other continents are becoming increasingly significant. This chapter explores Africa's relationships with the global community, the impact of the African diaspora, and Africa's evolving role in global geopolitics.

—-

Relationships with Other Continents: Trade, Politics, and Culture

1. Africa and Asia:

Trade and Investment:

Africa's trade relationships with Asia, particularly China, have grown rapidly in recent decades. China is now Africa's largest trading partner, with investments spanning infrastructure, mining, telecommunications, and energy sectors.

In addition to China, countries like India, Japan, and South Korea are also key players in African trade and investment. India, for example, is a major importer of African agricultural products, while Japan has made significant contributions to development in health and technology.

Belt and Road Initiative (BRI):

The BRI, launched by China, has led to large-scale infrastructure projects across Africa, including roads, railways, and ports. These investments have the potential to boost economic growth but have also raised concerns about debt dependency and the loss of sovereignty.

Cultural and Educational Ties:

Africa's cultural ties to Asia are also growing, with African music, fashion, and art gaining popularity in countries like China and Japan. In turn, African students are increasingly pursuing higher education opportunities in Asian universities, contributing to cross-cultural exchange.

2. Africa and Europe:

Colonial Legacy:

The historical relationship between Africa and Europe has been shaped by colonialism, which left enduring effects on Africa's political, economic, and social systems. European powers carved up Africa during the "Scramble for Africa" in the late 19th century, imposing arbitrary borders and exploiting the continent's resources.

Despite gaining independence, many African countries continue to face the legacy of colonialism in the form of economic dependency, political instability, and unequal trade relationships.

Trade and Economic Cooperation:

The European Union (EU) remains a significant trading partner for Africa. The EU provides preferential trade agreements through the Economic Partnership Agreements (EPAs), though critics argue these agreements often favor European interests.

Africa is an essential partner in the EU's efforts to combat illegal immigration, human trafficking, and terrorism. The EU has funded numerous development and humanitarian projects across Africa, particularly in the fields of health, education, and infrastructure.

Cultural Influence:

Africa's cultural footprint in Europe is growing, with African music, film, and literature receiving recognition at prestigious European events like the Cannes Film Festival and the Venice Biennale. African diaspora communities in Europe, particularly in the UK, France, and

Belgium, play a vital role in maintaining cultural ties and fostering mutual understanding.

3. Africa and the Americas:

Trade and Investment:

Africa's relationship with the Americas has been historically rooted in the transatlantic slave trade, which forcibly moved millions of Africans to the Americas. In modern times, the U.S. and Brazil are significant trade partners, with the U.S. investing in Africa's energy, agriculture, and infrastructure sectors.

African exports, including oil, minerals, and agricultural products, are critical to the economies of the U.S., Brazil, and other Latin American countries. In return, Africa imports technology, machinery, and manufactured goods from these regions.

The African Diaspora:

The African diaspora in the Americas, particularly in the United States, has been instrumental in shaping cultural, political, and social landscapes. From the civil rights movements to the global popularity of African-American music, the cultural contributions of the African diaspora are immeasurable.

The return of African-American communities to the continent, often referred to as "repatriation," has created ties between the African diaspora and the continent, as people reconnect with their ancestral roots.

Cultural Exchange:

African culture has had a profound influence on the Americas, particularly through music, food, dance, and fashion. Genres like jazz, hip-hop, and reggae have African origins and continue to shape global music trends.

Africa's growing creative industries, including film and fashion, are gaining recognition worldwide, particularly through events like the Pan African Film Festival in the U.S. and the growing influence of African fashion weeks in cities like New York, London, and Paris.

—-

The Impact of African Diaspora Communities Worldwide

1. Cultural Influence:

The African diaspora, which includes millions of people of African descent living outside the continent, has had a profound impact on global culture. From the music of the African-American community to the literature of Afro-Caribbean writers, the diaspora has been at the forefront of cultural movements and artistic expression.

African immigrants and their descendants have played pivotal roles in shaping the cultural fabric of countries across the globe, particularly in the Americas, Europe, and the Caribbean. The global influence of Afrobeat, hip-hop, and African cinema highlights the vibrant creativity that continues to flow from the African diaspora.

2. Political and Social Advocacy:

African diaspora communities have also been active in political and social advocacy. Movements like Black Lives Matter and the global push for racial justice and equality have their roots in the struggles faced by African communities throughout history.

Diaspora communities have formed powerful lobbying networks, advocating for African issues on the global stage. These include pushing for debt relief, foreign aid reforms, and more equitable trade practices.

African-Americans and Afro-Caribbean leaders, including activists like Marcus Garvey and W.E.B. Du Bois, have played key roles in advancing Pan-African ideals and fostering a sense of global African unity.

3. Economic Contributions:

The African diaspora is a major contributor to Africa's economy through remittances, which are a critical source of income for many African households. In 2022, remittances to sub-Saharan Africa totaled over $45 billion, surpassing foreign direct investment in some regions.

African entrepreneurs in the diaspora are also investing in businesses and startups across the continent, bridging the gap between Africa and the rest of the world.

—-

Africa's Role in Global Geopolitics

1. Africa's Growing Influence in Global Diplomacy:

As a key player in international organizations like the United Nations (UN) and the African Union (AU), Africa is playing an increasingly important role in global diplomacy. African countries have collectively pushed for reforms in global governance, including the restructuring of the UN Security Council to better reflect the continent's geopolitical significance.

Africa has been active in peacekeeping missions, conflict resolution, and mediating political disputes, both within the continent and globally. The AU's efforts in addressing crises in South Sudan, Somalia, and the Central African Republic have underscored Africa's commitment to peace and security.

2. Africa's Role in Climate Change and Sustainability:

Africa is a key player in global discussions about climate change. As the continent most vulnerable to the effects of climate change, Africa is advocating for more equitable climate action and financial support from developed nations.

African countries are at the forefront of renewable energy initiatives, including solar power projects and hydropower investments, with the potential to be global leaders in sustainable energy solutions.

3. Economic Powerhouse:

The African Continental Free Trade Area (AfCFTA), launched in 2021, has the potential to transform Africa into a unified economic powerhouse, boosting intra-African trade and attracting global investment.

Africa's natural resources, strategic location, and growing consumer markets make it an increasingly important player in global trade and geopolitics.

—-

Conclusion

Africa's relationships with the rest of the world are evolving. From economic partnerships to cultural exchanges, Africa is asserting its influence on the global stage. The African diaspora, with its cultural and economic impact, continues to strengthen ties between Africa and the world. As the continent becomes more integrated into global geopolitics, Africa is poised to play a central role in shaping the future of international diplomacy, trade, and cultural exchange. Through collaborative efforts, Africa's rising global influence can foster a more equitable and interconnected world.

Chapter 11: Challenges of Modern Africa

While Africa is on a path to growth and transformation, it faces numerous challenges that impede its progress. The continent grapples with complex issues such as unemployment, education gaps, health crises, ongoing conflicts, refugee displacement, and the effects of globalization. This chapter delves into these challenges, analyzing their root causes, impacts, and the efforts being made to address them.

—-

Unemployment, Education Gaps, and Health Crises

1. Unemployment and Underemployment:

Africa's rapidly growing population, particularly its youth, is a double-edged sword. While the continent's young demographic offers immense potential, it also exacerbates the challenge of creating enough jobs. According to the International Labour Organization (ILO), youth unemployment in sub-Saharan Africa remains one of the highest in the world, with millions of young people entering the labor market annually without sufficient job opportunities.

High unemployment rates, particularly among young people, fuel social unrest, poverty, and inequality. Many young Africans, particularly those in urban areas, are forced into the informal economy, where wages are low, job security is non-existent, and working conditions are often poor.

In rural areas, access to employment is even more limited, and many families depend on subsistence farming, which is vulnerable to climate change and market fluctuations.

2. Education Gaps and Quality:

Education is another critical area where Africa faces significant gaps. Although access to primary education has improved in many African countries, secondary and higher education remains a challenge. According to UNESCO, millions of children, particularly girls in rural areas, are still out of school, and those who do attend often face overcrowded classrooms and inadequate resources.

The quality of education remains a major concern. Many African schools lack qualified teachers, proper infrastructure, and modern learning materials. As a result, the education system struggles to equip students with the skills needed to succeed in a rapidly changing global economy.

In many parts of Africa, vocational and technical education is not prioritized, limiting opportunities for young people to gain practical skills that would prepare them for the workforce. Furthermore, the gap between education systems and the job market means that many graduates face high levels of underemployment or unemployment.

3. Health Crises:

Africa faces significant health challenges, from high rates of infectious diseases like malaria, tuberculosis, and HIV/AIDS, to the growing burden of non-communicable diseases such as diabetes, heart disease, and cancer.

Malaria remains one of the leading causes of death in Africa, with millions of people affected each year, particularly in sub-Saharan Africa. Although efforts to combat malaria, such as the distribution of insecticide-treated nets and access to antimalarial drugs, have made a difference, the disease remains a major public health issue.

HIV/AIDS continues to disproportionately affect many African countries, despite progress in treatment and prevention. While the number of new infections has declined, stigma, lack of access to healthcare, and inadequate education about the virus remain challenges in combating the epidemic.

In addition to infectious diseases, Africa is experiencing a rise in lifestyle-related health problems, exacerbated by urbanization, changing diets, and sedentary lifestyles. Access to quality healthcare remains limited in many areas, and there is a significant shortage of healthcare workers, particularly in rural regions.

—-

Conflict Zones and Refugee Challenges

1. Conflict Zones and Political Instability:

Africa has long been plagued by political instability and armed conflict. From civil wars in South Sudan, the Democratic Republic of Congo (DRC), and Somalia, to insurgencies in Mali, Nigeria, and the Sahel region, ongoing violence continues to disrupt economic development, displace millions of people, and cause humanitarian crises.

The root causes of conflict in Africa are often linked to ethnic tensions, political power struggles, corruption, and competition for resources. In many cases, these conflicts are exacerbated by external interference, the proliferation of weapons, and the breakdown of state institutions.

Political instability often leads to weak governance, corruption, and a lack of rule of law, which in turn worsens poverty, exacerbates social inequalities, and impedes efforts to achieve sustainable development.

2. Refugee and Displacement Crisis:

The displacement caused by armed conflict, human rights abuses, and environmental degradation has led to one of the largest refugee crises in the world. According to the United Nations High Commissioner for Refugees (UNHCR), Africa is home to millions of refugees and internally displaced persons (IDPs).

Countries like Uganda, Ethiopia, and Kenya host large numbers of refugees, primarily from neighboring conflict zones such as South Sudan, Somalia, and the DRC. These countries often struggle to provide adequate services and support to refugees, resulting in overcrowded camps, limited access to healthcare and education, and the risk of further displacement due to renewed conflict.

In addition to conflict-driven displacement, Africa also faces the challenge of environmental migration. Droughts, floods, desertification, and rising sea levels are driving rural populations to migrate, further intensifying the pressure on urban areas and creating a strain on resources and infrastructure.

—-

The Impact of Globalization

1. Economic Dependence and Trade Imbalances:

Globalization has had both positive and negative effects on Africa. On one hand, it has provided access to new markets, technologies, and investments. On the other hand, Africa's global trade relationships remain unequal, often resulting in the exploitation of its natural resources without adequate compensation or long-term benefits.

Africa remains heavily dependent on exports of raw materials—minerals, oil, agricultural products—while importing finished goods and services. This creates a trade imbalance and limits the potential for industrialization and economic diversification. The continent's reliance on commodity exports also makes it vulnerable to price fluctuations on global markets.

Many African countries have limited influence over international trade policies, often finding themselves at a disadvantage in global negotiations. Despite initiatives like the African Continental Free Trade Area (AfCFTA), intra-African trade remains relatively low compared to trade with the rest of the world.

2. Cultural Impact and Western Influence:

Globalization has led to the spread of Western culture, particularly through media, technology, and consumer goods. While this has introduced new ideas and modern conveniences, it has also contributed to the erosion of some traditional African values and cultural practices.

The proliferation of foreign media and the dominance of Western narratives have influenced the way many Africans see themselves and the world. This has led to the rise of a "globalized" youth culture that often prioritizes Western ideals over indigenous African traditions.

However, globalization has also allowed African culture to reach a global audience. African music, fashion, and film have gained worldwide recognition, and the rise of digital platforms has provided African artists and entrepreneurs with opportunities to showcase their talents on the global stage.

3. Technological Divide and Digital Inclusion:

While Africa has made significant strides in adopting technology, the digital divide remains a challenge. Rural areas often lack access to basic infrastructure like electricity and the internet, leaving large sections of the population excluded from the benefits of the digital age.

Access to technology is also unequal, with urban areas benefiting more from digital innovations, while rural communities face barriers such as high costs and limited connectivity. Bridging this gap is critical for Africa's continued development and participation in the global economy.

Additionally, Africa must address issues of data privacy, cybersecurity, and technological literacy to fully leverage the potential of the digital world. Increased investment in education, infrastructure, and tech startups will be crucial in ensuring that Africa does not miss out on the opportunities presented by the Fourth Industrial Revolution.

—-

Conclusion

Modern Africa faces significant challenges, but it is also a continent with immense potential for growth and transformation. Unemployment, education gaps, health crises, conflict zones, and the effects of globalization remain obstacles to progress. However, the resilience and determination of Africa's people, along with the commitment of governments, international organizations, and the private sector, can lead to solutions.

The path to overcoming these challenges lies in improving education systems, creating job opportunities, enhancing healthcare, resolving conflicts, and building resilient economies that can withstand the pressures of globalization. With strategic investments, collaboration, and a focus on sustainable development, Africa can tackle its challenges and realize its potential as a global leader in the 21st century.

Chapter 12: Africa's Cuisine

Africa's cuisine is as diverse and rich as the continent itself, with each region offering unique flavors, ingredients, and cooking techniques. The food of Africa is deeply intertwined with its history, culture, and traditions, serving not only as nourishment but also as a reflection of the social, economic, and spiritual fabric of society. In this chapter, we will explore some of the most iconic African dishes, the cultural significance of food traditions, and the growing influence of African cuisine on global food trends.

—-

A Tour of Flavors: Jollof Rice, Injera, Biltong, and More

1. Jollof Rice (West Africa):

Description: One of the most popular dishes in West Africa, Jollof rice is a fragrant, flavorful one-pot dish made with rice, tomatoes, onions, and a variety of spices. Variations exist across the region, with countries like Nigeria, Ghana, and Senegal each claiming their version of the dish.

Ingredients and Preparation: The base of Jollof rice is made from a blend of tomatoes, onions, and bell peppers, which are fried into a rich base before adding rice and stock. The dish is often cooked with meats like chicken, goat, or fish and flavored with ingredients like thyme, curry powder, and bay leaves. Some variations include adding vegetables like peas, carrots, and green beans.

Cultural Significance: Jollof rice is more than just a dish; it is a symbol of celebration and community. It is served at weddings, birthdays, and festive occasions across West Africa and is considered a comfort food.

The "Jollof rice wars" between Nigeria and Ghana reflect the pride both nations take in their recipe and preparation techniques.

2. Injera (Horn of Africa):

Description: A sourdough flatbread, injera is a staple food in Ethiopia, Eritrea, and other countries in the Horn of Africa. It is made from teff flour, a grain native to Ethiopia, and is known for its spongy texture and slightly tangy taste.

Ingredients and Preparation: Injera is traditionally prepared by fermenting teff flour with water for a few days, which creates its characteristic sour flavor. The batter is poured onto a large, flat griddle (called a mitad) to cook, resulting in a large, circular, porous flatbread.

Cultural Significance: Injera is often used as both a plate and an eating utensil. In Ethiopia and Eritrea, meals are commonly eaten communally, with injera placed on the table and covered with various stews and dishes. The bread's texture allows it to be used to scoop up meat, vegetables, and lentils, reflecting the importance of shared meals in African cultures.

3. Biltong (Southern Africa):

Description: Biltong is a dried and cured meat snack that originates from Southern Africa. It is similar to jerky but differs in its seasoning, preparation, and drying process.

Ingredients and Preparation: Typically made from beef, biltong is marinated in a mixture of vinegar, salt, sugar, and spices such as coriander, pepper, and cloves. The meat is then air-dried for several days, resulting in a flavorful, chewy snack.

Cultural Significance: Biltong is a popular snack in South Africa, Namibia, and Zimbabwe and is often enjoyed as a protein-rich treat during social gatherings or on long journeys. It has become a symbol of Southern African hospitality and is frequently offered to guests as a token of welcome.

4. Bunny Chow (South Africa):

Description: Originating in Durban, South Africa, bunny chow is a unique dish that consists of a hollowed-out loaf of white bread filled with curry. It is a fusion of Indian and South African cuisine, created during the Indian diaspora in the early 20th century.

Ingredients and Preparation: Traditionally filled with a spicy curry made from chicken, lamb, or beans, bunny chow is served in a portion of bread that forms a bowl around the curry. The bread soaks up the curry, adding to the dish's rich flavor.

Cultural Significance: The dish has become a popular street food, reflecting the multicultural influences in South Africa, particularly from the Indian community. Despite its humble origins as a takeaway meal for Indian laborers, bunny chow has become a beloved and iconic South African dish.

5. Piri Piri Chicken (Mozambique and Angola):

Description: Piri piri chicken, a dish popular in Mozambique and Angola, is known for its spicy kick, thanks to the piri piri chili. The chicken is marinated in a tangy, flavorful sauce made from garlic, lemon, oil, and the fiery chili, before being grilled or roasted.

Ingredients and Preparation: The sauce is made by blending piri piri chilies with lemon, garlic, vinegar, and oil to create a marinade. The chicken is coated in the sauce and left to marinate for several hours before being grilled or roasted, allowing the flavors to infuse the meat.

Cultural Significance: Piri piri chicken reflects the influence of Portuguese colonialism in Mozambique and Angola. The use of chilies, which are native to Africa, combined with European ingredients, showcases the fusion of African and European culinary traditions.

—-

The Cultural Significance of African Food Traditions

Food in Africa is not just about sustenance; it is deeply tied to cultural identity, family, and community. Across the continent, food is used to mark special occasions, celebrate heritage, and express social status.

1. Community and Family:

In many African cultures, meals are shared communally. Large platters of food are often served in the center of the table, and family and friends gather to enjoy the meal together. This communal aspect of eating fosters bonds within families and communities, with food serving as a medium for connection and conversation.

For example, in West Africa, it is common for families to eat from a single bowl of rice or stew, with each person using their hands to scoop up the food. This tradition emphasizes the values of unity and sharing.

2. Rituals and Ceremonies:

Food plays an important role in African rituals and ceremonies, whether it's a wedding, a birth, a religious holiday, or a harvest festival. For instance, in some African cultures, certain foods are prepared to honor ancestors, gods, or spirits during religious ceremonies. These rituals often involve the offering of food as a sign of respect or a request for blessings.

Special dishes are often reserved for specific events, such as the preparation of fufu and goat stew during weddings in parts of West Africa or the making of nyama choma (grilled meat) for family reunions in East Africa.

3. Symbolism and Identity:

Many African foods are symbolic of local identity and heritage. In Ethiopia, for example, the communal eating of injera signifies the collective nature of Ethiopian society. Similarly, Jollof rice has become a symbol of West African pride, representing the region's culinary diversity and its ability to adapt and innovate.

Food is also used as a means of preserving cultural traditions, passing recipes down through generations, and maintaining a connection to the past. In many rural areas, traditional cooking methods are still used, including open fires and earthenware pots, which not only add flavor but also preserve ancient culinary techniques.

—-

Fusion Cuisine and Africa's Influence on Global Food Trends

1. Globalization of African Flavors:

As the world becomes more interconnected, African cuisine is gaining popularity beyond the continent's borders. In cities across the world, African restaurants are becoming increasingly common, with chefs highlighting dishes like Jollof rice, injera, and piri piri chicken on global menus.

The growing interest in African flavors is partly driven by the African diaspora, whose culinary traditions have been shared with the world through migration, trade, and the rise of social media. The fusion of African flavors with other cuisines is also on the rise, as chefs experiment with ingredients and cooking techniques from both Africa and other parts of the world.

2. Modern African Fusion Cuisine:

African fusion cuisine is a growing trend in global culinary circles. This style blends traditional African ingredients and dishes with influences from European, Asian, and American cuisine. For example, a contemporary twist on Jollof rice might incorporate avocado, a popular ingredient in many other parts of the world, or be paired with gourmet meats such as Wagyu beef.

Another example is the fusion of African and Mediterranean flavors, seen in dishes like Moroccan tagine served with couscous and African spices like berbere, or African-inspired tacos with spicy grilled meats and pickled vegetables.

3. Global Food Movements and African Influence:

African cuisine is also playing a key role in global food movements, such as the increasing emphasis on plant-based diets. African staples like legumes (beans, lentils) and grains (millets, sorghum) have long been part of the traditional African diet and are gaining popularity for their health benefits and sustainability.

In the field of sustainable food practices, African agriculture is leading the way with techniques like agroecology and traditional farming methods that emphasize biodiversity, soil health, and the use of indigenous crops. These practices are inspiring chefs and food activists around the world who are advocating for a return to more sustainable and locally sourced food.

—-

Conclusion

Africa's cuisine is a rich tapestry of diverse flavors, techniques, and cultural practices that reflect the continent's history, traditions, and people. From the savory spices of Jollof rice to the tangy bite of injera, African food is a celebration of community, heritage, and creativity. As the world becomes more interconnected, Africa's culinary influence continues to grow, with its flavors becoming an integral part of global food culture. The fusion of traditional African dishes with international flavors is creating exciting new possibilities, ensuring that Africa's food traditions remain relevant and continue to evolve on the global stage.

Chapter 13: Arts and Entertainment

Africa's artistic expression through music, dance, fashion, and cinema is as diverse and vibrant as the continent itself. From ancient traditions to modern global recognition, African arts have played a crucial role in shaping not only the continent's cultural identity but also its influence on the world. This chapter explores the evolution of African music, dance, and fashion, along with the rise of Nollywood, South African cinema, and the growing prominence of African artists on the global stage.

—-

The Evolution of African Music, Dance, and Fashion

1. African Music: From Traditional Rhythms to Global Soundscapes

Traditional Foundations: African music has its roots deeply embedded in the continent's various cultures. Each ethnic group has its own musical traditions, with instruments such as drums, mbiras, xylophones, and stringed instruments playing central roles in African music. These instruments are not merely entertainment tools but are often used in rituals, ceremonies, and communal activities, carrying deep spiritual and cultural meanings. The use of rhythm is central to African music, reflecting the heartbeat of life, and is used to tell stories, preserve history, and celebrate moments of joy.

The Rise of Modern African Music: With the introduction of Western instruments and the blending of local sounds, modern African music began to take shape in the 20th century. Genres like highlife from West Africa, and juju music from Nigeria, saw the fusion of traditional African rhythms with jazz, blues, and funk. Afrobeat, pioneered by Fela Kuti, emerged as a genre combining traditional African rhythms with funk, jazz, and political activism, quickly gaining a global audience. By the 1980s and 1990s, hip hop, R&B, and reggae had found a home in Africa, evolving into distinct subgenres like hip-hop, Afrobeat, and dancehall.

Global Impact: Today, African music is not just a cultural expression but a global phenomenon. Artists such as Burna Boy, Wizkid, Tiwa Savage, and Yemi Alade have put African sounds on the world stage, dominating global charts and collaborating with international stars. Afrobeats, a genre that blends pop, hip-hop, and traditional African rhythms, has become one of the most influential genres in global music today. International festivals and global streaming platforms, such as Spotify and Apple Music, have amplified African music's reach, bringing it into mainstream consciousness worldwide.

2. Dance: The Heartbeat of African Culture

Traditional Dance: Dance has been integral to African culture for centuries. African dances are diverse, varying from region to region, tribe to tribe, and community to community. These dances are used for ritualistic purposes, storytelling, celebrations, and as a form of communal unity. The movement in African dance is often energetic, rhythmic, and fluid, reflecting the spiritual connection to the earth and ancestors. For example, the traditional dances of the Zulu people, characterized by strong, powerful movements, contrast with the more flowing and graceful movements of dances in East Africa.

Contemporary African Dance: With the advent of modern influences and global exposure, African dance has evolved to incorporate hip-hop, jazz, and electronic dance styles. In the 21st century, dances like the Azonto from Ghana, Shaku Shaku from Nigeria, and Gwara Gwara from South Africa have gained international fame, showcasing Africa's ability to blend its traditional movements with contemporary influences. Social media platforms like TikTok and Instagram have further pushed African dance trends into the global spotlight, with millions of people worldwide participating in viral dance challenges.

Cultural Expression: Dance remains a central part of African identity, used to convey emotions, experiences, and cultural history. Whether it's the popular Afrobeats dance moves or the traditional dances performed at cultural festivals, African dance continues to influence global dance trends, shaping how the world perceives African creativity and style.

3. Fashion: A Fusion of Tradition and Modernity

Traditional Fashion: African fashion is an expression of identity, pride, and cultural heritage. Each region in Africa has its own traditional clothing, often crafted from locally sourced fabrics such as kente from Ghana, shweshwe from South Africa, and ankara from West Africa. These garments often carry symbolic meanings, with patterns and colors representing different clans, beliefs, or occasions. For example, in West Africa, the brightly colored kente cloth is worn during significant ceremonies and celebrations, symbolizing royalty and prestige.

The Rise of Contemporary African Fashion: In recent decades, African designers have taken the world stage by storm, blending traditional fabrics and techniques with contemporary styles. Designers like Oumou Sy, Duro Olowu, and Thebe Magugu have showcased their collections at major international fashion weeks, proving that African fashion can compete with the best in the world. These designers often incorporate African prints and textiles into global fashion trends, giving traditional fabrics a modern twist and allowing Africa to influence global fashion trends.

African Fashion's Global Influence: African fashion has gained significant global recognition, with African designers making a mark in luxury markets and mainstream fashion. Events like Africa Fashion Week in London and the South African Fashion Week showcase the continent's diverse creativity and emerging talent. African-inspired fashion has become a statement of pride and identity, with global celebrities such as Beyoncé, Michelle Obama, and Rihanna donning African designers, cementing African fashion's place in international haute couture.

—-

Nollywood, South African Cinema, and Other Media Industries

1. Nollywood: Africa's Cinematic Powerhouse

A Global Industry: Nollywood, Nigeria's film industry, is one of the largest and most influential in the world. With over 2,500 films produced annually, Nollywood has become the second-largest film industry globally in terms of output, just behind Bollywood. What makes Nollywood unique is its rapid production pace, low-budget filmmaking, and its focus on themes that resonate with African audiences, such as family, love, politics, and societal issues.

The Growth and Popularity of Nollywood Films: Nollywood films, often made in local languages such as Yoruba, Igbo, and Hausa, have captured the attention of African diaspora communities across the world. These films are widely distributed on DVDs, television channels, and streaming platforms, making them accessible to a global audience. Nollywood's international reach has expanded through collaborations with Hollywood stars and global distributors, such as Netflix, which has featured a growing catalog of Nigerian films.

Key Nollywood Films and Stars: Films like The Wedding Party, Lionheart, and Half of a Yellow Sun have garnered international acclaim, while actors such as Genevieve Nnaji, Omotola Jalade Ekeinde, and Richard Mofe-Damijo have become household names across Africa and beyond.

2. South African Cinema: A Global Narrative

Historical Context: South African cinema has evolved from its historical context, marked by the struggles against apartheid and the transition to democracy. Early South African films such as Cry, the Beloved Country (1951) addressed issues of racial segregation and injustice, while more recent works have focused on post-apartheid reconciliation and the nation-building process.

International Success: South African filmmakers have gained global recognition through films like Tsotsi, which won an Academy Award for Best Foreign Language Film in 2006, and District 9, a science fiction film set against the backdrop of apartheid. These films have showcased South Africa's unique storytelling approach, blending local history and culture with universal themes of inequality, freedom, and social justice.

The Role of South African Cinema in Global Geopolitics: South African cinema continues to have a significant role in shaping global narratives around race, identity, and resistance. The country's film industry reflects the diverse cultures of South Africa and explores the complexities of post-apartheid society.

3. Other Emerging African Film Industries

East African Cinema: Countries such as Kenya, Uganda, and Tanzania have seen a rise in film production, with filmmakers like Wanuri Kahiu (Rafiki) and Mira Nair (The Namesake) making their mark on international cinema. The development of new film schools and the rise of digital technology have contributed to the growth of cinema in East Africa, making it a promising region for global audiences.

North African Cinema: Countries like Egypt, Tunisia, and Morocco have long-standing traditions in cinema, with Egypt being the home of the Arab world's first film industry. Contemporary filmmakers such as Youssef Chahine and Nouri Bouzid have used their films to explore social issues within the Arab world and North Africa, helping these films gain recognition at prestigious international festivals like Cannes and Venice.

—

Global Recognition of African Artists

1. The Global Influence of African Music:

Worldwide Reach: Artists like Burna Boy, Wizkid, and Angelique Kidjo have gained international acclaim, performing at major international music festivals and collaborating with artists from various genres, including Beyoncé, Drake, and Ed Sheeran. The global rise of Afrobeats, a genre blending traditional African rhythms with pop and dancehall, has led to increased interest in African music, influencing global charts and the music industry's landscape.

2. Visual Artists Making Their Mark Globally:

African Contemporary Art: African artists are also making waves in the global art scene. Artists like El Anatsui, Yinka Shonibare, and Ibrahim Mahama have showcased their work in major galleries and museums worldwide. These artists blend traditional African materials with contemporary techniques, addressing themes of colonialism, identity, and globalization in their work.

Art Fairs and Auctions: Events like the 1:54 Contemporary African Art Fair in London and auctions at Christie's and Sotheby's have brought African art into the international spotlight. The growing market for African art signifies the increasing recognition and appreciation of the continent's creative expression.

—-

Conclusion

Africa's arts and entertainment sectors have experienced a remarkable evolution, from traditional music and dance to the rise of Nollywood, South African cinema, and global recognition of African artists. African creativity has transcended borders, contributing significantly to the world's cultural landscape. The global influence of African music, dance, fashion, and cinema continues to grow, shaping trends and redefining the way the world perceives Africa's rich and diverse cultural heritage. Through the arts, Africa's voice is not only heard but also celebrated on the world stage.

Chapter 14: The Youth of Africa

Africa is a continent defined by its youth, with over 60% of its population under the age of 25, making it the youngest continent in the world. This dynamic demographic serves as a double-edged sword: on one hand, it holds immense potential for economic, social, and political transformation; on the other hand, it presents challenges that require deliberate policies and investment. In this chapter, we explore the role of Africa's youth as both an asset and a challenge, their engagement with education, social media, and activism, and their leadership in youth-driven movements for societal change.

—-

Africa's Young Population: An Asset and a Challenge

1. The Asset of Youthful Energy

Demographic Dividend: With such a youthful population, Africa has a unique opportunity to harness the "demographic dividend." This refers to the economic growth potential that arises when there is a larger proportion of the working-age population. Countries like Kenya and Ghana are already beginning to reap the benefits, with young entrepreneurs leading the charge in industries like technology and agriculture.

Innovation and Creativity: Young Africans are at the forefront of innovation. From tech hubs in Nairobi and Lagos to creative industries in Johannesburg, they are reshaping traditional sectors and spearheading new ones. Startups like M-Pesa, Andela, and Flutterwave are examples of youth-led initiatives transforming African economies.

2. The Challenge of Unemployment

High Youth Unemployment Rates: Despite their potential, millions of African youths face unemployment or underemployment. According to the African Development Bank, the unemployment rate for young people in Africa is often twice as high as that of older populations. Limited job creation and skills mismatches exacerbate the issue.

Urban Migration and Overcrowding: Young people are increasingly moving to cities in search of opportunities, leading to overcrowded urban centers. This urbanization, if not managed well, strains infrastructure and creates socio-economic inequalities.

3. The Risk of Disenfranchisement

Frustration and Discontent: Unmet aspirations can lead to social unrest. In some cases, disenfranchised youth become vulnerable to radicalization, crime, or migration through dangerous routes in search of better opportunities.

Political Marginalization: Despite forming the majority of the population, young people are often excluded from key decision-making processes. This lack of representation in leadership roles adds to their frustrations.

—-

Role of Education, Social Media, and Activism

1. Education as a Catalyst

Improving Access: Access to primary and secondary education has improved significantly over the past few decades, but challenges remain in providing quality education and bridging gaps in higher education.

Skills for the Future: Many African youths are graduating with degrees that do not align with job market needs. Investment in technical and vocational education, as well as STEM fields (Science, Technology, Engineering, and Mathematics), is crucial for equipping young people with skills for emerging industries.

Educational Innovators: Young Africans are leveraging technology to democratize education. Platforms like Eneza Education and uLesson provide affordable, accessible learning tools for students across the continent.

2. The Power of Social Media

Connecting Youth Across Borders: Social media has become a powerful tool for young Africans to connect, share ideas, and collaborate. Platforms like Twitter, Instagram, and TikTok amplify their voices and allow them to engage with global audiences.

Digital Advocacy: Social media has enabled youth to organize and advocate for change. Campaigns like #FeesMustFall in South Africa and #EndSARS in Nigeria were born and gained momentum on digital platforms, showcasing the power of online communities in driving real-world change.

Cultural Influence: Young Africans are using social media to promote and celebrate their cultures, from music and fashion to food and language. This digital presence is reshaping global perceptions of Africa.

3. Youth-Led Activism

Political Movements: Young people across Africa have been at the forefront of political activism, demanding accountability, transparency, and justice from their governments. Examples include protests against police brutality in Nigeria and student-led movements for affordable education in South Africa.

Climate Action: Africa's youth are leading the charge against climate change. Activists like Vanessa Nakate from Uganda are raising awareness about Africa's vulnerability to climate crises and calling for global climate justice.

Community-Based Initiatives: Beyond protests, many young Africans are driving change at the community level, launching initiatives that address local issues like clean water access, education, and healthcare.

—-

Youth-Led Movements for Social and Political Change

1. Case Studies of Youth Movements

#EndSARS (Nigeria): This youth-led movement against police brutality highlighted the power of young Nigerians to mobilize and demand systemic change. It drew international attention and forced the government to disband the controversial SARS unit.

#FeesMustFall (South Africa): This student-led movement called for the reduction or elimination of university fees, highlighting issues of inequality in higher education. It successfully pressured the government to increase funding for tertiary education.

African Youth Climate Movement: Young environmentalists across the continent are organizing protests, lobbying governments, and participating in global climate summits to advocate for sustainable policies and practices.

2. Youth in Governance

Demanding Representation: Across Africa, young people are calling for more representation in governance. Movements like "Not Too Young to Run" in Nigeria have successfully lowered the age requirements for political office, empowering more youth to participate in leadership.

Entrepreneurship in Politics: Some young Africans are bypassing traditional political pathways to create change by starting businesses, NGOs, and social enterprises that address critical issues like healthcare, education, and technology access.

—-

The Way Forward

Africa's youth hold the key to the continent's future. For this potential to be realized, governments, private sectors, and civil society must prioritize investments in education, job creation, and political inclusion. Initiatives that foster entrepreneurship, digital literacy, and leadership skills can transform Africa's youth from a challenge into the driving force behind a prosperous and equitable continent.

—-

Conclusion

The youth of Africa embody the continent's hope and resilience. With their energy, creativity, and determination, they are breaking barriers and shaping the future of Africa in profound ways. From driving political change to leading innovations in technology and sustainability, Africa's young people are not just the leaders of tomorrow—they are the leaders of today. Their journey is not without challenges, but their spirit and potential ensure that Africa's future remains bright and full of promise.

Chapter 15: The Spirit of Africa

Africa is more than just a continent—it is a mosaic of cultures, traditions, and histories woven together by the unifying threads of resilience, community, and humanity. Despite its challenges, Africa's enduring spirit lies in its people's ability to adapt, innovate, and thrive. This final chapter explores the essence of Africa's spirit, captured in themes like ubuntu, resilience, and community, and celebrates the continent's beauty, strength, and diversity. Finally, it calls for unity, collaboration, and sustainable development as Africa steps confidently into the future.

—-

The Spirit of Ubuntu: Humanity Towards Others

Ubuntu, a Nguni Bantu term meaning "I am because we are," encapsulates the essence of African values. It emphasizes interconnectedness, compassion, and mutual support—principles that have guided communities for centuries.

1. Community-Centered Living

In African societies, individuals are viewed as part of a collective. Families, extended families, and villages work together to ensure everyone's well-being. This communal way of life has been a cornerstone of survival and prosperity across the continent.

Ubuntu fosters a sense of duty toward others. Whether in times of celebration or crisis, communities come together, demonstrating solidarity that transcends borders.

2. Ubuntu in Modern Times

Ubuntu continues to influence leadership, governance, and social movements. Leaders like Nelson Mandela invoked the spirit of ubuntu in their calls for reconciliation and unity, showcasing its power to heal and build.

In today's interconnected world, ubuntu is reflected in how Africans engage with global challenges, from advocating for climate justice to supporting peacebuilding efforts.

—-

Resilience in the Face of Adversity

Africa's history is marked by triumphs over immense challenges, from colonial exploitation to contemporary struggles with poverty and inequality. Resilience is deeply embedded in the continent's identity.

1. Historical Resilience

Despite centuries of colonization, African societies preserved their cultures, languages, and traditions. Post-independence movements demonstrated the continent's determination to reclaim its sovereignty and dignity.

2. Modern Examples of Resilience

Communities have adapted to environmental challenges like droughts and floods by developing innovative agricultural practices and sustainable technologies.

In the face of health crises such as the HIV/AIDS epidemic and Ebola outbreaks, African nations have shown remarkable unity, innovation, and determination to rebuild.

3. The Power of the African Spirit

Resilience is evident in Africa's creative industries, where musicians, filmmakers, and artists tell stories of hope, strength, and perseverance.

It is also seen in the entrepreneurial spirit of young Africans who, despite limited resources, build businesses, create jobs, and drive economic growth.

—-

Diversity and Beauty: A Continent of Contrasts

Africa's diversity is unparalleled. From its landscapes to its people, the continent offers a rich tapestry of beauty and culture that deserves celebration.

1. Cultural Diversity

With over 3,000 ethnic groups and more than 2,000 languages, Africa is a testament to human creativity and adaptability. Each culture brings unique traditions, art, and wisdom that contribute to the global human experience.

Festivals, music, and dance are powerful expressions of African identity, showcasing the continent's vibrancy and joy.

2. Natural Wonders

Africa's landscapes are as diverse as its people, ranging from the vast Sahara Desert to the lush Congo rainforest, and from Mount Kilimanjaro to the majestic Victoria Falls. These natural wonders are a source of pride and inspiration.

The continent is home to unparalleled biodiversity, with wildlife and ecosystems that are critical to the planet's health.

3. Culinary Heritage

African cuisine, rich in flavors and history, reflects the continent's agricultural bounty and cultural diversity. From the spicy stews of West

Africa to the grilled delicacies of Southern Africa, food is a celebration of life and community.

—

A Call for Collaboration and Sustainable Development

As Africa moves forward, its spirit of community and resilience must guide efforts toward collaboration and sustainability.

1. United for Progress

The African Union's Agenda 2063 outlines a vision for a prosperous, peaceful, and integrated continent. Achieving this vision requires unity among nations and a shared commitment to addressing common challenges.

Regional collaborations, such as the African Continental Free Trade Area (AfCFTA), demonstrate the potential for economic growth through partnership.

2. Sustainability as a Core Principle

Africa's natural resources are its greatest assets, but they must be managed responsibly. Sustainable practices in agriculture, energy, and tourism can ensure that future generations benefit from the continent's wealth.

Young Africans are leading the charge in environmental conservation and green innovations, providing hope for a sustainable future.

3. Global Collaboration

Africa's spirit of ubuntu extends to its relationships with the rest of the world. The continent seeks partnerships based on mutual respect, equality, and shared goals, rejecting exploitative models of the past.

By working together, Africa and the global community can address pressing issues such as climate change, inequality, and health crises.

—-

The Future of Africa's Spirit

The spirit of Africa is unbreakable. It lies in the stories of individuals who rise above challenges, in the songs of joy and hope that echo across the continent, and in the shared dreams of a brighter future.

As Africa's youth embrace the values of ubuntu, resilience, and community, they carry forward the legacy of their ancestors while forging new paths. Their creativity, determination, and vision ensure that Africa will continue to thrive and inspire the world.

—-

Conclusion: A Celebration of Africa

The spirit of Africa is a beacon of hope, a testament to humanity's ability to overcome adversity and find strength in diversity. As the continent looks to the future, it must draw upon its rich heritage and collective will to build a sustainable, inclusive, and prosperous society.

Africa's story is one of beauty, strength, and possibility. By embracing its spirit and working together, the continent can unlock its full potential and inspire the world to do the same.

Copyright Page

For permission requests, please contact the author directly at [skiesonlinemedia@gmail.com].

First Edition: 2024

Published by Tawanda Tawanda

Contact skiesonlinemedia@gmail.com

Printed in Africa.

Don't miss out!

Visit the website below and you can sign up to receive emails whenever Tawanda Tawanda publishes a new book. There's no charge and no obligation.

https://books2read.com/r/B-A-JMDYC-ZRLLF

BOOKS 2 READ

Connecting independent readers to independent writers.

Also by Tawanda Tawanda

Life After Divorce
African Child
Purpose of Life
Africa

About the Author

I am Tawanda Tawanda, a 36-year-old man born and raised in the vibrant country of Zimbabwe. Growing up in this beautiful land, I have always been deeply connected to its rich culture, history, and people. From the vast savannas to the bustling urban centers, Zimbabwe shaped me into the person I am today—someone who values resilience, community, and faith.

My journey has been one of growth, learning, and overcoming challenges. Life has never been without its obstacles, but it has always been a journey full of lessons, both the difficult and the joyful. I have always believed that each experience, whether positive or painful, is an opportunity to grow, and this perspective has shaped both my personal life and my outlook on the world.

Early Life and Background

Born in Zimbabwe, I was raised in a family that cherished the importance of community, family bonds, and strong ethical values. The warmth of our culture, where we were taught the significance of respect for one another, the value of hard work, and the centrality of faith, influenced my core beliefs and principles.

Growing up, I faced a unique set of challenges—some of which were universal, and others that were deeply personal. Zimbabwe's economic challenges and political landscape certainly shaped my youth, and they fostered in me a deep sense of resilience. At the same time, my family, faith, and the friendships I formed over the years played a crucial role in shaping my identity.

I have always been drawn to stories—whether through books, music, or shared experiences. It was through these stories that I learned the power of hope, healing, and renewal. This love of stories later led me to pursue writing as a way to share my journey and the lessons I have learned.

A Journey of Faith and Growth

Throughout my life, I have been on a spiritual journey that has shaped not just my personal experiences, but also my understanding of love, loss, and purpose. Faith has been the anchor through the storms of life. It was through the teachings of Scripture, my community of believers, and the wisdom passed down from elders that I discovered how to truly lean on God in moments of difficulty.

My faith has also been tested. Like many, I have faced personal trials, including the painful experience of divorce.

www.ingramcontent.com/pod-product-compliance
Lightning Source LLC
LaVergne TN
LVHW041039150826
845672LV00001B/389

* 9 7 9 8 2 3 0 9 9 1 1 8 2 *